CHRISTMAS JOKES FOR KIDS

ORCHARD

ORCHARD BOOKS

First published in Great Britain in 2024 by Hodder & Stoughton

5 7 9 10 8 6 4

Text copyright © 2024 Hodder & Stoughton Limited.
Illustrations copyright © 2024 Hodder & Stoughton Limited.

Illustrations by Dynamo Limited

Additional images © Shutterstock

A CIP catalogue record for this book
is available from the British Library.

ISBN 978 1 40837 310 1

Printed and bound in Great Britain by
Clays Ltd, Elcograf S.p.A

The paper and board used in this book
are made from wood from responsible sources.

MIX
Paper | Supporting
responsible forestry
FSC® C104740

Orchard Books
An imprint of
Hachette Children's Group
Part of Hodder & Stoughton Limited
Carmelite House
50 Victoria Embankment
London EC4Y 0DZ

An Hachette UK Company
www.hachette.co.uk

www.hachettechildrens.co.uk

What happens to naughty elves?
They get the sack.

**Knock, knock!
Who's there?
Noah.
Noah who?**

Noah good Christmas joke?

What do snowmen eat for breakfast?

Snowflakes.

Why did Rudolph have to go to summer school?

Because he went down in history.

What is a Christmas tree's favourite shape?

A Treeangle!

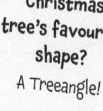

5

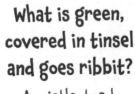

What is green,
covered in tinsel
and goes ribbit?

A mistle-toad.

What diagnosis did
the doctor give to the
patient who kept eating
Christmas decorations?

Tinsellitis.

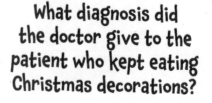

Where do Santa's
elves go swimming?

The North Pool.

How do sheep say Merry
Christmas to each other?

Fleece Navidad.

What type of music
do elves like?

Wrap music!

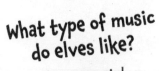

What is the name of
Father Christmas's dog?

Santa Paws!

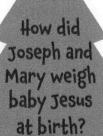
How did Joseph and Mary weigh baby Jesus at birth?

They had a weigh in the manger.

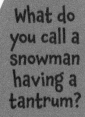
What do you call a snowman having a tantrum?

A meltdown.

Why are elves such great public speakers?

They have plenty of elf-confidence.

What game do reindeer play at sleepovers?

Truth or deer.

What do elves say when Santa takes the register?

Present!

What did the football commentator get from Santa Claus?

COOOOOOOAAAALLL!

Knock, knock!
Who's there?
Elf.
Elf who?
Elf me wrap
this present!

What month do
Christmas trees
hate the most?

Septimber!

What do you call Father
Christmas when he
stops moving?

Santa Pause.

How much did Santa pay for his sleigh?

Nothing. It was on the house!

What goes "Oh, Oh, Oh"?

Santa walking backwards!

How do the elves clean Santa's sleigh on the day after Christmas?

They use Santatiser.

Knock, knock!
Who's there?
Mary.
Mary who?
Mary Christmas!

What is a Christmas tree's favourite sweet?

Ornamints!

What do you call a cat sitting on the beach on Christmas Eve?

Sandy Claws.

Why does everyone love snowmen?

They're cool.

What do you get when you cross a Christmas tree with an apple?

A pineapple!

What do you call an elf wearing earmuffs?

Anything you want – they can't hear you!

Why don't aliens celebrate Christmas?

Because they don't want to give away their presence.

Knock, knock!
Who's there?
Donut.
Donut who?

Donut open this present until Christmas!

What happened to the thief who stole an Advent calendar?

He got twenty-five days in jail.

Why is Christmas the coldest time of year?

Because it's in Decembrrrr!

Where does Santa keep all his money?

At the snow bank.

How does Rudolph know when Christmas is coming?
He refers to his calendeer.

What do you call a sheep that doesn't like Christmas?
Baaa humbug!

What do you get when you cross a snowman and a vampire?
Frostbite.

15

What do Santa's
elves like to eat?

Elfabet soup!

What falls but never gets hurt?

Snow.

What do elves do
after school?

Their gnomework.

16

What do you call an old snowman?
Water.

What do gingerbread men use when they break their legs?
Candy canes.

What do you call a greedy elf?
Elfish.

17

What did one snowman say to the other?

Do you smell carrots?

What's the weather report every Christmas Eve?

There's a one hundred per cent chance of rein-deer.

How do snow globes feel?

A little shaken.

18

Who delivers presents to sharks?

Santa Jaws.

What's red, white and blue at Christmas?

A sad candy cane.

What Christmas carol do cranberries sing?

"We Wish You a Berry Christmas".

19

How do you make a Christmas tree laugh?

Tickle its mistletoes.

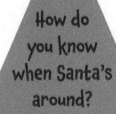

How do you know when Santa's around?

You can always sense his presents.

What did the stamp say to the Christmas card?

Stick with me and we'll go places.

What do you sing at a snowman's birthday?
"Freeze a Jolly Good Fellow".

What's the most festive herb?
Christmas thyme.

What did Santa say on Christmas morning?
That's a wrap!

I can always predict what's inside a Christmas present.

It's a gift.

Why couldn't Santa find anyone to help with his gifts?

No one was present.

How many presents can Santa fit in an empty sack?

Just one. After that, it's not empty!

Why does a broken drum make a good Christmas present?

You can't beat it.

Did you hear about the Christmas tree sale?

It was a tree-for-all.

Why is a foot a good Christmas gift?

It fits perfectly in a stocking.

What's the scariest thing about the holidays?
The ghost of Christmas presents.

What do you get if you cross Santa with a duck?
A Christmas quacker.

What do snowmen call their kids?
Chilldren.

What do snowmen wear on their heads?
Ice caps.

What do you call a
pigpen in winter?
A pigloo.

Where do elves
go to vote?
The North Poll.

What do you call Santa's
least polite reindeer?
Rude-olph.

Did Rudolph
go to school?
No, he was elf-taught.

Which of Santa's
reindeer are
dinosaurs
afraid of?
Comet.

Why are Christmas
trees so fond of
the past?
Because the present's
beneath them.

What's a reindeer's favourite game?
Stable tennis.

How do you get into a reindeer's house?
Ring the deerbell.

What do reindeer hang on their Christmas trees?
Hornaments.

27

Why doesn't Santa eat junk food?
Because it's bad for your elf!

Why doesn't Santa go to the hospital?
He has private elf care.

What athlete is warmest in winter?
A long jumper!

Where would you find
a snowman dancing?

At a snowball!

Why do mummies like
Christmas so much?

Because of all
the wrapping!

Why can't penguins fly?

They're not tall enough to be pilots.

29

What did Rudolph have to say about a big book of noses that Santa gifted him?

I already red that one.

What do you call someone who can't stop talking about last Christmas?

Santamental!

What do you get when you cross Santa with a detective?

Santa Clues!

30

What do snowmen enjoy most at school?
Snow-and-tell!

What does an elf study in school?
The elfabet.

What did Santa say at the start of the race?
Ready, set, ho ho ho!

What's the difference between the Christmas alphabet and the regular alphabet?

The Christmas alphabet has Noel.

What do monkeys sing at Christmas?

"Jungle Bells"!

What do snowmen eat for lunch?

Icebergers.

What does Mrs Claus use to bake cakes?

Elf-raising flour.

What does Santa eat for breakfast?
Mistle toast.

Why does Santa go down the chimney?
Because it soots him.

Did you know Santa Claus is good at karate?
It's true. He has a black belt.

What do you get if you put a bell on a skunk?

Jingle smells.

Knock, knock!
Who's there?
Justin.
Justin who?

Justin time for Christmas presents!

What did one Christmas ornament say to the other?

Wanna hang out?

How does Santa check the weather report?

On the winternet.

Who hides in the bakery at Christmas?
A mince spy.

How do snowmen get around?
They ride an icicle.

What do you call an elf who has just won the lottery?
Welfy.

How does Christmas
Day always end?
With the letter "y".

What kind of ball
doesn't bounce?
A snowball!

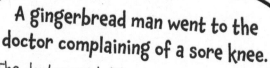

A gingerbread man went to the
doctor complaining of a sore knee.
The doctor said, "Have you tried icing it?"

What do you call a
snowman party?
An icebreaker!

My friend just won the tallest
Christmas tree competition.
I thought to myself, *How can you top that?*

What did the third wise man say after his friends had presented gold and frankincense?

But wait, there's myrrh!

Why did the gingerbread man go to the doctor?

He was feeling crumby!

Why did the snowman call his dog Frost?

Because Frost bites!

What makes a candy cane a collector's item?
When it's in mint condition.

Who delivers Christmas presents to elephants?
Elephanta Claus.

Why wouldn't the Christmas tree stand up?
It had no legs.

What kind of photos do elves take?
Elfies!

What did one snowman say to the other?
Chill out.

What do fish sing during the holidays?
Christmas corals.

39

Why was the snowman looking through a bag of carrots?

He was picking his nose!

What do the elves call it when Father Christmas claps his hands?

Santapplause!

What did Santa's dog ask for this Christmas?

A mobile bone.

What's as big as Santa
but weighs nothing?
Santa's shadow!

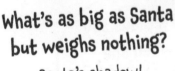

What do you call a reindeer
on Halloween?
A cariBOO!

Who is Santa's
favourite singer?
Elfis Presley.

What's an elf's favourite sport?
North Pole-vaulting.

Why didn't the turkey eat anything at Christmas?
Because it was stuffed.

What did Mrs Claus say to Santa when she looked up at the sky?
Looks like rein, deer!

What's the difference betwe
Santa's reindeer and a knigh
One slays the dragon, the other drags the sleigh.

What do snowmen take when the sun gets too hot?

A chill pill.

How do you keep all the Christmas dinner food locked up and safe before Christmas day?

You use a tur-key!

Did you know that Santa's not allowed to go down chimneys this year?

It was declared to be too dangerous by the elf and safety team.

What's a snowman's favourite food?

Chilli.

Why does your nose get tired in winter?

It runs all day.

Why was the gingerbread man robbed?

Because of his dough.

Where do you find reindeer?

It depends on where you leave them.

How does Father Christmas measure the size of presents?

In santametres.

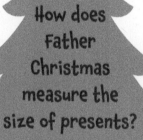

Why do basketball players love gingerbread biscuits?

Because they can dunk them!

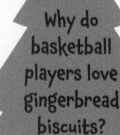

45

What do you call a
snowman in the desert?
A puddle.

Did you hear about the fake
Santa visiting the zoo?
Turns out he was a cheetah.

Why was the Christmas
turkey in a rock band?
Because it was the only
one with drumsticks!

What do dogs sing
at Christmas?
"Bark! The Herald Angels Sing"

What did the snowman say to the robin?

I have snow idea!

Why did the turkey cross the road?

Because it wasn't chicken.

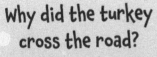

Who do Santa's helpers call when they're ill?

The national elf service.

What do you call a penguin in the desert?

Lost.

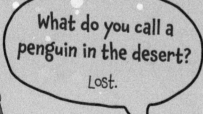

Why did the elf fall down the chimney?
Because they slipped . . .

Why did the second elf fall down the chimney?
Because they were holding the first elf's hand . . .

Why did the third elf fall down the chimney?
Because they thought it was a game!

What do you call Father Christmas when he's telling jokes?

Banter Claus.

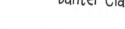

What do you call Father Christmas when he hasn't cut his fingernails?

Santa Claws.

I love Christmas jokes.

They just keep giving.

I went to the doctor and she said I have an addiction to telling Christmas jokes.

Other than that, I'm in good elf.

What did the snowflake say to the fallen leaf?

You are so last season.

What do you get when you cross a crocodile with a snowman?

A cold snap.

What do angry mice send each other at Christmastime?

Cross mouse cards.

50

What do you get when you cross a pig and a Christmas tree?

A porcupine.

What did the family sing when they retired their Christmas tree?

"Fir He's a Jolly Good Fellow".

What do you call cutting down Christmas trees?

Christmas chopping!

What did one
Christmas tree
say to the other?
Lighten up!

Why did the Christmas
tree go to the doctor?
It was feeling green.

How much money
do elves get paid?
Sacks full.

Why did the chicken
cross the road on
Christmas Eve?
To get out of the way
of Santa's sleigh!

Why was the snowman lonely?

Because he lived in a snow globe by himself.

How do snowmen chill their drinks?

They just put them in their pockets.

Why are Christmas trees bad at knitting?

They always drop their needles.

What treat do snowmen enjoy the most?

Snow cones.

Why did the gingerbread man run so fast?

He had a sugar rush.

Why did the gingerbread man have to buy a new house?

Because the kids ate the last one.

What do gummy sweets sing at Christmas?

'Tis the season to be jelly!

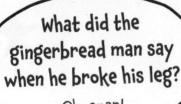

What did the gingerbread man say when he broke his leg?

Oh, snap!

What do you call a baby snowman?

A snowball.

Why do mice celebrate Cheesemas instead of Christmas?

Because it's a holey day!

Why did the piece of paper not want to go to the Christmas dinner?

Because it was afraid of par-snips!

What do holly bushes say to each other at Christmas?

Happy hollydays.

Why did the Christmas tree love the Christmas lights?

Because they lit up its life.

Why do abominable snowmen get the most Christmas presents?

Because their Christmas stockings are huge!

What do elves do in school?

Presentations.

Why don't prawns give gifts on Christmas?

Because they're shellfish.

What did one gingerbread man say after all the others were eaten?

It's hard to bake new friends.

What did the sea say to Santa
as he flew over in his sleigh?

Nothing. It just waved.

What did the salt say to
the pepper at Christmas?

Seasoning's greetings.

What goes
ho ho thump?

Santa laughing
his head off.

Someone must be
mad at the snowman . . .

because they gave
him two black eyes.

59

What did one mince pie say to the other?
Nothing. Mince pies can't talk.

How does Good King Wenceslas like his pizza?
Deep pan, crisp and even.

Why do cats take so long to wrap Christmas presents?
They want them to be purrfect.

Why do insects hate Christmas?
They're humbugs.

Why do penguins swim in saltwater?
Because pepper makes them sneeze.

What did one angel say to the other?
Halo there.

When does Christmas come before Halloween?

In the dictionary.

What did the mummy present say to the baby present?

Wrap up warm.

How do you feel when you can't get to your Advent calendar chocolate?

Foiled.

Why is everyone so thirsty at the North Pole?
No well, no well.

Where does mistletoe go to become famous?
Holly wood.

What do you call people who are scared of Christmas?
Claus-trophobic.

What did the dog say at Christmas dinner?

Bone appétit.

What do sheepdogs say at Christmas?

Happy collie days!

What treats do dogs get for Christmas?

Candy canines.

64

Why shouldn't you leave a dog outside at Christmas?

They might turn into a pupsicle.

Where can you find dogs at Christmas?

Dachshund through the snow.

What do dogs chase at Christmas?

Jingle balls.

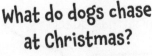

Why are Santa's helpers so good at making things?

They love Do-It-Your-Elf!

Did you hear about the girl who fell into a Christmas pudding?

She was dragged in by a strong currant.

What do ducks do before Christmas dinner?

Pull their Christmas quackers!

What does Santa do when the reindeer pull the sleigh too fast?

Hold on for deer life.

What kind of sea creatures do they have at the North Pole?

Jollyfish.

What should you do if your car breaks down on Christmas Eve?

Get a mistletow.

How much do polar bears weigh?

Enough to break the ice.

Knock, knock!
Who's there?
Woo.
Woo who?
Wow, you're really
excited about Christmas!

What sound
does a turkey's
phone make?
Wing-wing.

Which dinosaur
loves Christmas
the most?
Tree rex!

Why did the
Christmas tree
go to the dentist?

It needed a root canal.

Why did the
snowman go
to the dentist?

To fix his
frostbite.

Why did the
mince pie go to
the dentist?

It needed a filling.

**What did the
beaver say to the
Christmas tree?**

Nice gnawing you.

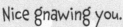

What do you call a running turkey at Christmas?

Fast food.

**Why couldn't the pony sing
the Christmas carols?**

Because it was a little horse.

The Christmas pudding, yule log and mince pies went on strike this year.

They weren't pudding up with this any longer.

Doctor, doctor! I've got a Christmas pudding stuck up my nose!

I'll give you some cream for that.

What do gingerbread men sleep on?

Baking sheets.

71

Why did all the other polar bears call one polar bear lazy?
It always did the bear minimum.

Would you like to buy Rudolph and his brother?
No thanks, they're two deer!

How do cats greet each other at Christmas?
Meow-y Christmas!

Why does Santa always use a map?
He doesn't want to be a lost Claus.

Why is Santa out of work?
Because he was given the sack.

Why do reindeer wear bells?
Their horns don't work!

Where do cats like to go at Christmas?
Whisker Wonderland.

Why do birds fly south for Christmas?
It's too far to walk.

Why was there no Christmas cake left at the shop?

Because they were stollen.

Where do reindeer go if they lose a tail?

The retail store.

What did the policeman say when he saw a snowman stealing?

Freeze!

What do snowmen put on their dinners?
Chilli sauce.

What do you call a snowman with no arms or legs?
A snowball.

How do you invite Santa to a party?
You request his presents.

75

Why did the snowman get detention?

He was up to snow good.

How do you keep track of how many mince pies you've eaten?

With a mince pie chart.

What did the dinosaur say when it was Christmas Eve?

Merry T. rexmas.

What's white and goes up?

A confused snowflake.

What did one Christmas pudding say to the other?

You're on fire!

Why can't you shock reindeer?

They've herd it all.

What do cows say to each other at Christmas?
Moooey Christmas!

How do snowmen travel?
On a snowmobile.

What will you be at Christmas after eating dessert?
Yule be happy.

Why did one polar bear fall in love with the other?
He thought she was beary pretty.

Why do reindeer tell
such good stories?
Because they all have tails.

What do you call a
pair of candy canes?
Sugar chums.

When is a Christmas
pudding musical?
When it's piping hot.

What was the librarian's favourite Christmas song? "Silent Night".

How do you make a mince pie fall asleep? Sing it a lulla-pie.

What do you have in December that you don't have in any other month? The letter "D".

When does a reindeer have a trunk?

When it goes on holiday.

Why did Santa put a clock in his sleigh?

Because he wanted to see time fly.

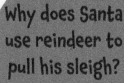

Why does Santa use reindeer to pull his sleigh?

Because moose can't fly.

What do you call a polar
bear with no teeth?

A gummy bear.

Why do people drink eggnog at
Christmas?

Because it's eggs-tra special.

What did the yule log say
when it was cut into slices?

Yule be sorry!

What does Santa say when he
gets back to the North Pole after
delivering all the presents?

Ho ho home sweet home.

What's invisible and smells like milk and cookies?

Santa's burps.

Where do little mince pies go?

Pie-mary school.

Why did the elves keep breaking their bones?

They were Santa's brittle helpers.

Which side is left of a Christmas pudding?

The side that hasn't been eaten.

What do you call a great
Christmas decorator?
A mistlepro.

What sound do birds make on Christmas morning?
Season's tweetings.

What do you call a half-man,
half-horse that delivers
presents at Christmas?
Centaur Claus.

What do construction workers
put on their Christmas dinner?
Crane-berry sauce!

What do you call a grumpy Christmas fairy?

A sour plum fairy.

What do Santa's elves do at parties?

Have wrap battles.

How do you stop a reindeer from smelling?

Hold its nose.

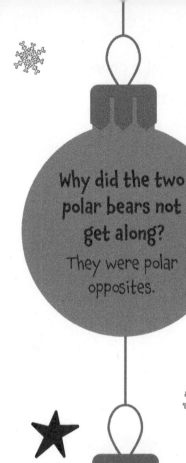

Why did the two polar bears not get along?
They were polar opposites.

How does Mrs Claus deliver her cookies?
In a gingerbread van.

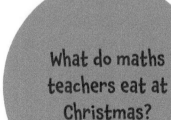

What do maths teachers eat at Christmas?
Mince Pi.

What do bodybuilders eat at Christmas?
Muscle sprouts.

Why did the snowman paint itself with a highlighter?
It wanted to glow, man.

Which animals at the North Pole are best at maths?
Braindeer.

Why did the eggnog make everyone laugh?

It was a practical yolker!

What do you call reindeer poos?

Yule logs.

What do you call a paper snowflake?

A snowfake.

Why did Scrooge put his clock in the bank?

To save time.

Why did Scrooge put his wallet on ice?
He likes cold hard cash.

What do scientists do on Christmas Eve?
They decorate the chemistree.

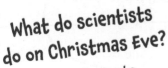

How do Santa's elves find missing presents?
With a nut-tracker.

What's the best thing to put into a Christmas pudding?
Your teeth.

What is white, furry and has wheels?
A roller bear.

Why should you always have a ladder with you when you go Christmas carolling?
To reach the high notes.

There was only one yule log left at the shop.
I thought, *Yule do.*

What do zombies put on their Christmas dinner?
Grave-y.

What did one mince pie say to the other?
I only have pies for you.

What kind of wreaths do fish hang
on their door at Christmas?

Coral wreaths.

Why did the elves put
their beds in the woods?

They wanted to sleep like logs.

Why couldn't the Christmas
caroller come inside?

They couldn't find the right key.

What kind of Christmas tree do turkeys have?
A poul-tree.

What's red and white and goes up and down?
Santa stuck in a lift.

What is red and white, red and white and red and white again?
Santa Claus rolling down a hill.

What can you catch in winter but not throw?
A cold.

I had a candy cane joke but I've forgotten it.
It's on the tip of my tongue.

Why was the Christmas tree's friend so sad?
It was a weeping willow.

What's a ghost's favourite part of Christmas dinner?

Mince pie with scream.

What do you call a girl who's always singing Christmas hymns?

Carol.

In what year does Christmas Day and New Year's Day fall in the same year?

Every year.

How do you know when a snowman is unhappy with you?

It will give you the cold shoulder.

What kind of key can't open a door?

A tur-key.

Why was the snowman so well travelled?

It had seen all of the snow globe.

What's a secret agent's favourite Christmas carol?

"Spy-lent Night".

What did the Christmas tree wear to keep warm?

A fir coat.

More hilarious joke books ...

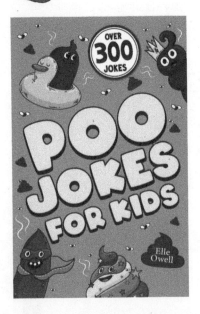
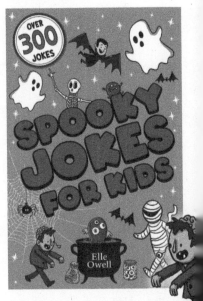